Meditation Starts With ME

Meditation Starts With ME

The Secret of Sitting Still and Enjoying Meditation

Gwen Peterson

DEDICATION

As I reflect on the early days of my journey a few teachers come to mind. Esther Hicks, Louise Hay, Wayne Dyer, Deepak Chopra and Jack Boland. I AM grateful for how their work supported me.
May you find yours.

CONTENTS

ACKNOWLEDGMENTS

Sometimes we get the inspiration to write a book. We feel it in our hearts but we allow ourselves to be distracted for many reasons.
Thank you, Sandra and Angel, for being part of my accountability writing group. Your love and support kept me on track to get this book published.

1
UNLOCKING THE SECRET

We've all been there—we hear the word *meditation* and it conjures up images of yogis sitting in the lotus position or monks retreating to caves for lifetimes. I bet you've tried meditation yourself and you gave yourself a big *FAIL*.

I can hear you now:

"Why is meditation so important, anyway Gwen? It seems like such a waste of time."

or

"It's too hard. I can't sit quietly. My mind is too busy. It's too hard to find the time. It's just... too hard."

How do I know? I've been there. I know the internal struggle that bubbles up at the mere mention of the word *meditation*. I felt it when I first started, and I've heard it from my students for decades since.

I hear you. I really do. I have uttered these words myself. When I began my meditation practice, I struggled, too. I didn't understand what meditation was, why it mattered, and most importantly, why it felt so difficult. With patience and determination, I discovered the truth about meditation—what it is, what it *isn't*, and what it *can* do for you.

Since then, I've guided thousands of people toward creating a successful meditation practice for themselves. I write this book now to help you create a lasting meditation practice and discover parts of you that have been hidden by the noise and distractions of life.

Here's the thing: a meditation practice is like learning to ride a bike. It's a journey of balance and persistence. And just like riding a bike, you don't know *how* until you get on it and ride.

You won't be perfect right out of the gate. You might fall off or stop for a little bit but pick it up and start again. Soon you will look forward to the benefits of meditating and understand that each experience is unique and different. You will discover a depth to your life you couldn't have imagined.

2
WHY MEDITATE?

Let me start by asking you this: Without a meditation practice, do you know when you are quiet enough to hear all the thoughts swirling around in your head?

Go ahead, guess.

If your answer is: W*hen I go to bed.* You're right!

Are you finding it hard to fall asleep quickly and easily? If so, you're not alone. Most of the time when someone can't fall asleep it's because their mind won't quiet down and that's a sure sign—it's time to start a meditation practice.

Meditation is the best form of self-care both mentally and physically. Did you know, meditation has been linked to countless health benefits? Maybe you are exploring meditation right now because of health reasons.

Thorpe and Dasguta[1] discuss how meditation can:

- Reduce stress
- Control anxiety
- Promote emotional health
- Enhance self-awareness
- Lengthen attention span
- Reduce age-related memory loss
- Help fight addictions
- Improve sleep

- Manage pain
- Lower blood pressure

That is a lot of health benefits. I think most folks start their meditation practice to reduce stress or anxiety only to find out that meditation touches all areas of their life.

And here's some food for thought: according to Pew Research[2], 40% of Americans meditate at least once a week, and of those, 70% have been doing so for less than two years. If that many people are giving it a try, why not you?

Already tried but can't make it work? Read on. I can help you.

3
MY MEDITATION JOURNEY

Let me share how it started for me. Maybe you can relate and be hopeful.

Picture this: I was living life by the book—school, college, career, house, husband, dog, kid. Check, check, and check. Everything was supposed to lead to happiness, right? But it didn't. Despite doing everything by the book, I felt hollow. Empty. Like something vital was missing, and I couldn't quite put my finger on it.

I kept hearing about meditation—how it could fill the void, calm the mind, and bring peace. But as a corporate multitasking Type-A personality, the idea of sitting still for ten minutes made no sense. I could do so much in ten minutes! Sitting and doing *nothing* went against every fiber of my being. But that void inside pushed me to try.

This was way before YouTube and other social media platforms and I was not sure where to start. My favorite inspirational teachers at the time were Jack Boland, Wayne Dyer and Deepak Chopra so I experimented with their guided meditation tapes and CDs.

I found I would fall asleep quite often and decided to do my meditation at bedtime and found my sleep was so much better. Then I began silent meditations for 10 minutes, on Mondays, Wednesdays, and Fridays.

It was easier for me to stick to my routine if I did it first thing in the morning before my day filled up with stuff to do or became distracted by the drama of the day.

Let me stress to you that my mind fought back every inch of the way. I felt like I was doing everything wrong. Yet at the same time something surprising happened: I began to enjoy the downtime. My sleep was improving. I felt calmer. Encouraged by the results, I upped my practice to Monday through Friday, giving myself the weekends off as a reward.

It didn't take long to notice a pattern. My weekdays were calm and productive, but by Monday morning, after a meditation-free weekend, my mind and life were chaotic. The lightbulb moment came: Was it the meditations making the difference? Had to be. From then on, I committed to a daily practice and experimented with different types of meditation.

4
WHY IS MEDITATION DIFFICULT?

Behind the excuses of not enough time, feelings of wasting time and you must be doing something wrong, is *the mind*.

The mind is the thing that talks to you all day and all night, if you let it. Studies say we have upwards of 6,000 thoughts per day. Whew! That's a lot of thoughts. Those thoughts tend to be fearful by default as a result of being fed a pretty consistent diet of fear from our daily living. You probably haven't given much thought to those thoughts and you are not alone.

We have also been conditioned to think we have no control over our minds and what we think. This is false. We have control over our minds. We lack the fortitude to keep it in check and that is where meditating comes in. Through your meditation practice you will get to know your mind, the thoughts you have and the opportunity to change those thoughts. As a result, you will become less fearful, more happy and more peaceful when times get tough.

The mind is the whole reason for meditation. I won't go into the spiritual end of the mind but if you feel you need to go deeper into your practice, check out my books, *Insights & Illuminations: A Trilogy to Unleash Your Playful Soul and Transform Your Life* and *It's A Game, Winning With Spirit: The Ultimate Life Strategy*.

Be aware your mind will not go along willingly.

Nobody's does. The mind likes to be in control and run the show, good or bad. That is why when someone says they can't quiet their mind, I applaud them. They have accomplished so much with that statement. It takes a certain amount of awareness to even realize they can't quiet their mind. It is from that awareness the meditation practice will bloom.

For parents or pet owners, I think you will know what I mean when I say it requires a lot of stick-to-itiveness when training your child or puppy. Let your guard down and you will undo a month of training. There can be a lot of kicking and screaming or puppy dog eyes but with a little perseverance you see the fruit of your labor. Your mind is like that child or pet.

Let's think about a bedtime ritual as meditation. You want your child (mind) to go to sleep (quiet down to meditate) but instead you get pushback. There is a lot of guff. You have a choice. Stand firm and it will ultimately pass or buckle and the next round will be even harder.

That, my friends, is meditation. When you are starting out you will be taming the unruly child (mind). You aren't doing anything wrong. You are doing everything right. You have just met your mind and are noticing how it has been running the show the whole time.

No fear. As we move through this book, you will see how to regain control and move deeper into your meditation practice.

5
TYPES OF MEDITATION

Meditation is about consciously focusing the mind. Focusing it on the present moment. Not the future or past. Not the day's drama. Instead, directing your mind to stay on point. A point *you* give it. Not letting it drift off onto tangents of thought.

Who is the *you* I am referring to? The observer part of you. Your higher self if you will. The part of you that never grows old. The one doing the noticing and the watching.

Your practice will take time and some mental acrobats. That is why this is a practice. Each day will be different. Each day will hold treasures. Be ready to discover things about yourself you never knew.

Over the years, I've explored different meditation styles, each with unique ways to focus. Each accomplishing something a little different. Below I describe the different types you can use. Play with them. Discover which ones will best suit your needs for that day's practice.

Mindfulness

Focus is placed on something specific. Here are some examples.

- Inhalation and exhalation of breath. Breathe in

to the count of 4, exhale to the count of 4 using full belly breaths.

- Notice sounds without engaging in thought.
- Count to 40 without having an interruption of thought. Start over if your mind steps in. If 40 is too difficult start with 10 and increase from there.
- Focus on an object. Such as a candle, flower or music.
- Notice thoughts as they come and go, but don't engage.

Mantra

Use a phrase or word to anchor your attention. It can be a Sanskrit mantra, a loving-kindness affirmation, or an inspirational quote. Repeat it mindfully, connecting deeply with the words as you think or speak them aloud. Another way is to listen to a pre-recorded mantra meditation of your choosing.

Guided

Also known as visualization, this involves following a narrator's cues to imagine calming scenes, like walking through a serene forest or sitting by a bubbling brook. Guided meditations are the best when first start out. You may find it is easier to keep your mind focused and visualization has a powerful effect on your life experience.

Chakra

Focus is placed on the body's energy centers. Root, Sacral, Solar Plexus, Heart, Throat, Third Eye and Crown being the main ones. This practice aims to clear, balance, and energize these points. I recommend a guided meditation focused on chakra clearings to get started.

Yoga

Traditional yoga integrates breath and movement, embodying mindfulness in motion. Hatha yoga is especially focused on this powerful connection between breath and body.

Stop here and listen to what you are already hearing. Is there any pushback? Take a moment and write them down here. Don't judge just listen and observe.

6
BUILDING YOUR PRACTICE

Meditation doesn't need to feel overwhelming. To be successful you must feel comfortable with your practice. It may even require a little negotiating with yourself at the beginning. Remember my weekends off scenario.

Let's begin looking at creating your practice.

1. **Commit**

   Begin with a manageable plan, it can be as simple as meditating once a week. Build from there as you go. Commitment is key—your mind will rebel like a toddler testing their boundaries. Stay firm.

2. **Schedule**

   Pick a day and time. Add it to your calendar to prioritize it. Hint: Now that it is on your calendar, don't be surprised when everything seems to fall on that day at that time. Again, stay firm. Reschedule those other things. It's a law of attraction thing. Stop here and do it now.

3. **Create**

   Find a quiet, distraction-free spot. Bedroom or bathroom. A room with a door is best when starting out. Maybe make a sign letting people know to not disturb you. This will become your Sacred Space.

4. **Comfort**

Being comfortable is more important than aesthetics—sit in a chair, lie down, or sit cross-legged if it feels good. In time, add the other stuff like incense, crystals and such. For now, keep it simple. Do you have a space now? Take a look at it. Sit down and imagine yourself sitting there. How does it feel?

5. **Choose**

Decide on the type of meditation you want to work with. Earlier I discussed the different meditations available. Decide which one you will start out with and have it ready for the big day. Have no idea where to start. I have free meditations on my YouTube channel. I have the links at the end of the book under Resources. Have one ready to use **before** your scheduled meditation. Test them out to see if they feel good to you.

7
NOW YOUR PRACTICE STARTS

Here we go!! It's the big day. You are in your sacred space, in your comfy position and ready to play your meditation audio/video.

WAIT! Before you push that button, remind yourself of these points below. I want you to be successful at this. I want you to be ready for the small child (the mind) who is not necessarily happy about this.

1. **Breathe**

   Start with three deep breaths, signaling your body to relax and your mind to focus. Inhale deeply into your belly, then exhale fully.

2. **Observe**

   Your mind will wander—that's natural. Notice where it goes without engaging. Meditation isn't about stopping thoughts; it's about observing them. Don't judge.

3. ***All* of this is part of the practice**.

   If you're new to meditation, be prepared: your mind will get very active, no matter the type of meditation you choose. It's going to chatter—loudly.

It might judge you and you may hear: Am I doing this right? I'm not doing this right! Why are we even doing this? We have better things to do.

You might suddenly remember the junk drawer that *needs* organizing right now. You'll get a laundry list of "urgent" tasks to tackle right now.

Your job is to gently remind your mind that you are sitting for ten minutes, stay firm. Notice what keeps coming up—it's valuable insight into your mental landscape.

I can't say it enough. Meditation is a practice, every day will feel different. Some will be peaceful. Others will be noisy. Whatever comes up, the goal remains the same: be present with it. Hear it but don't engage. Observe.

4. **Remember, meditation is about focusing.** Focusing on the present moment, not the past or future. Observing where your mind is. Is it hyped up or calm, happy or sad? How does your body feel? If something feels uncomfortable, adjust—stretch or change your position. Notice sensations like the air on your skin or the relaxation of your muscles. Noticing but not engaging.

Now it is time to start. Push the button and begin your journey. I hope you are excited.

8
WHEN THE MIND REFUSES TO FOCUS

Sometimes, your mind won't cooperate. It will kick and scream. It will demand attention, often pulling at something emotionally charged in your life. What then?? Huh Gwen? What then?? I did everything you said and I feel like I'm losing this battle.

PERFECT! LOOK AT YOU! You are truly developing your awareness and doing everything right. Even if it doesn't *feel* like it. The icky feeling you may be having is cognitive dissonance. The peacefulness you feel on a deeper level coming into conflict with the thoughts that don't align. This is the moment when you begin to change your life.

Here is my remedy for an unruly child. **Listen to it.**

Your mind wants to be heard. We spend all day everyday shutting down thoughts we don't want to think about. Maybe this is why you've been lying awake until 3 a.m., unable to shut your thoughts off.

When your child won't focus, it's time to bring in another tool: journaling. Writing down what's on your mind can help release it and give you the clarity to return to your meditation practice. Let the act of journaling be a companion to your journey, allowing space for the thoughts that are demanding your attention.

Remember, I spoke about the fearful default setting we have. Those persistent thoughts that nag at you night and day, need to be heard in their entirety before they will quiet. That's right. More times than not, once these thoughts are written down and looked at for what they are, they quietly go away or inspire you to take-action in a meaningful way. Can these old thoughts be replaced with something more in alignment with your deeper self? Let yourself feel the relief.

What are you hearing now? Take a moment and write.

9

THE PRACTICE OF SELF-LOVE

Meditation is the ultimate act of self-love and care. It's a space to hear your thoughts, feel your body, and simply *be*. Through meditation, you'll cultivate calm, clarity, and a newfound sense of control. And as your practice deepens spiritually, so will the benefits—both in your mind and in your life. Maybe you can feel a warmth come up in your heart center as you read these words.

I have found many of my students are caregivers of one sort or another. They take care of the needs of others before they take care of their own. This can lead to health issues and an unbalanced life. This is why starting your meditation practice is so powerful. It is the opportunity to recharge your batteries, even better than sleep can. It gives you the strength and power to be available to those you care for; in a way that simply pushing through your day can.

Struggling to figure things out? Stop and listen to yourself and look at what you truly want from your life. What do *you* want. Not what others are demanding of you.

Meditation isn't about being selfish. It's about having the love, energy and clarity to continue caring for those who are important in your life.

Gwen, can 10 minutes a day be that important? Can it make such a big change in my life and health?

Only one way to find out.

Sit your butt in a chair for 10 minutes!

I say smiling.

10
RESOURCES I'VE CREATED TO SUPPORT YOUR JOURNEY

You probably noticed I have been doing this for quite some time. I have worked with thousands of people in discovering themselves through meditation. Over time, I have recorded meditations and classes and written books. I offer weekly Insights and Illuminations, an inspirational email, to encourage exploring your true self.

Meditation and journaling are the foundation for any spiritual practice. Although you may have come to this book to find relief from a stressful life, it won't be long before you discover the true beauty of this practice. The magic it holds in creating a life that is amazing on a level you didn't realize could exist.

Explore these resources. Use the ones that speak to you. This is your journey to create. Enjoy.

Much love and gratitude,

Gwen

Insights and Illuminations website:
https://www.insightsandilluminations.com

Facebook:
https://www.facebook.com/insightsandilluminations

Instagram:
https://www.instagram.com/insightsandilluminations

YouTube:
https://www.youtube.com/@insightsandilluminations

Meetup:
https://www.meetup.com/insights-illuminations/

Learn More:
https://www.insightsandilluminations.com/learn-more-links/

My Author's Page:
https://www.amazon.com/author/insightsandilluminations

11
FINAL THOUGHTS

As I am putting the final touches on this book and contemplating, did I cover everything I can with you so you can find the magic and the peace that I have found with meditation, it occurred to me that not only is this sentence way to long but I failed to mention a point you may not hear by those teaching meditation.

As you settle into your meditation practice and begin to find the peaceful alignment with your Soul/heart center begin to hold onto that feeling throughout the day.

Not the out of body aspect of your practice but rather the calmness and observer.

It will take some time to finesse this. At first, it may be for 5 minutes before someone snaps you out of alignment. That's okay. The win here is that you noticed you left that alignment. Take a moment and see if you can realign.

You may be wondering why on earth (pun intended) would you ever want to do this, at this point simply starting your practice is a big enough hurdle. Well, when you are finding your alignment and holding onto it, your life changes before your eyes.

You are no longer engaged in the drama unfolding and you are able to navigate it like a guru. People will take notice that you don't react quite the same way to stressful situations. People will ask how you do it.

You will have taken back control of your life in a new and magnificent way. You will find yourself living a life that you are quite content with. Things come easily to you and you smile more often for no reason at all.

My Meditation Goal

Start Date:

Goal:

Why:

Type of Meditation:

Action Plan: Day and Time

Notes to Self:

REFERENCES

1   Matthew Thorpe and Raj Dasgupta, "Benefits of Meditation: 12 Science-Based Benefits of Meditation," Healthline, October 2020, https://www.healthline.com/nutrition/12-benefits-of-meditation. Accessed 21 September 2022

2   David Masci and Conrad Hackett, Meditation Common Across Many U.S. Religious Groups," Pew Research Center, 2 January 2018, https://www.pewresearch.org/fact-tank/2018/01/02/meditation-is-common-across-many-religious-groups-in-the-u-s/. Accessed 21 September 2022

Meditation Starts With ME

ABOUT THE AUTHOR

Gwen is an internationally known spiritual teacher, Reiki Master and author who has dedicated herself to inspiring and guiding others to live in harmony, healing and peace. Gwen is a Soul coach and mentor and has had the honor of supporting countless people in their own awakening and ascension process. As a conscious channel, Gwen is a conduit for the Divine. Her work is a reflection of her own personal journey of spiritual empowerment. She believes we are all capable of living our most authentic and joyful life. In addition to being the Creator of Insights and Illuminations, she is the Founder of Spiritual Communities Network, a global community of teachers and seekers of spiritual growth. She has been featured in Natural Awakenings Magazine, and on numerous podcasts.

Meditation Starts With ME